LUDWIG VAN BEETHOVEN

VIOLIN CONCERTO

D major/D-Dur/Ré majeur
Op. 61

Edited by
Richard Clarke

Ernst Eulenburg Ltd

London · Mainz · Madrid · New York · Paris · Prague · Tokyo · Toronto · Zürich

CONTENTS

The present edition of Beethoven's Violin Concerto Op. 61 is based on the relevant
texts published in *Ludwig van Beethoven : Werke : neue Ausgabe sämtlicher Werke*, III/4.

Ernst Eulenburg Ltd
48 Great Marlborough Street
London W1F 7BB

PREFACE

Beethoven's Violin Concerto in D major has long been regarded as one of the greatest challenges in the solo violin repertoire: a test of artistic maturity as much as technical command, and thus a work which every virtuoso worthy of the name should master at some point in his or her career. So it comes as a surprise to discover how coolly it was received at its first performance in Vienna on 23 December 1806. The composer Carl Czerny, a great admirer of Beethoven, may have been guilty of wishful thinking when he reported that the concerto 'was produced with very great effect'.[1] In all likelihood the applause was more for the soloist, the brilliant Franz Clement, who virtually sight-read the hugely difficult, and almost certainly much-corrected violin part with great aplomb, and who added a dazzling improvisation of his own (apparently holding the violin upside-down at one point) between two of the movements. The general reaction to Beethoven's music is probably better summed up by a review in the Viennese *Zeitung für Theater, Musik und Poesie* dated 8 January 1807:

As to Beethhofen's [sic] concerto, the verdict of the cognoscenti is unanimous: they concede that it has some beauty, but maintain that the continuity often appears completely broken, and that the endless repetition of some commonplace passages can easily prove wearisome. They assert that Beethhofen could put his undoubtedly great talents to better use, and present us with works like his symphonies in C and D, his delightful Septet in E flat […]

This opinion, or something like it, seems to have prevailed for nearly four decades, during which performances of the Violin Concerto barely rose into double figures. It was only when the 13-year-old Joseph Joachim – destined to become one of the 19th century's legendary violin virtuosos – played it at a concert in London in 1844, with Mendelssohn conducting, that the concerto's outstanding qualities at last began to be recognized by the wider musical public.

What Beethoven thought of Clement's performance is not recorded, but it is possible that his feelings are reflected in the otherwise unexplained change to the concerto's dedication. The first page of the autograph is inscribed, with a characteristically heavy Beethovenian pun: 'Concerto par Clemenza pour Clement primo Violino e direttore al theatro a vienna' [Concerto with clemency for Clement, first violin and director at the theatre in Vienna]. But when the score was published in 1808, it bore a dedication to Beethoven's childhood friend Stephan von Breuning. It is also worth noting that Beethoven never gave any evidence of wanting to write another violin concerto, and that his production of violin sonatas also tails off markedly after 1806. Nine sonatas for violin and piano – the last of which is the famous 'Kreutzer' Sonata, Op. 47 No. 4, of 1802–3 – appeared before the concerto; after it Beethoven composed only one solo violin work, the Sonata in G, Op. 96 (1812, rev. 1815). The latter is widely counted one of Beethoven's finest chamber works with piano, but the violin writing is markedly less virtuosic, more in a lyrical contemplative vein, than in either the 'Kreutzer' Sonata or the outer movements of the Violin Concerto.

Apart from Carl Czerny, there was at least one other early encouraging voice with regard to the Violin Concerto. In April 1807, Beethoven was visited by the pianist, composer and head of a London publishing firm, Muzio Clementi, who was anxious to secure the English rights for some of Beethoven's latest works. These included the Fourth Piano Concerto, Op. 58, the three 'Razumovsky' string quartets, Op. 59, Symphony No. 4, Op. 60, and the Overture *Coriolan*, Op. 62. From his correspondence it appears that Clementi singled out the Violin Concerto for special praise; but he also made

[1] Carl Czerny, *Pianoforte-Schule*, Op. 500, IV, 117

what with hindsight seems a strange request: would Beethoven also make an arrangement of the Violin Concerto for piano and orchestra? This duly appeared, with the same opus number as the violin version, and bearing a dedication to Stephan von Breuning's wife Julie. Arrangements of concertos for other solo instruments were by no means uncommon in the 18th and early 19th centuries, but the re-working of the violin part of Op. 61 – which was almost certainly made by someone else on Beethoven's behalf, following a few suggestions scribbled on the autograph by the composer – did nothing to rescue the concerto's reputation. It is, in fact, a remarkably unimaginative, sometimes downright clumsy adaptation, in which the left hand does little more than accompany the right hand's leading line. The intricate or dramatic interplay between the hands, so typical of Beethoven's solo style in his five numbered piano concertos, is almost entirely lacking.

In any case, this initially attractive deal with Clementi eventually turned sour. By the end of 1809 none of the above-mentioned works had appeared in print in England, and no payment had been forthcoming. Clementi, still working on the Continent, was eventually roused to fury on Beethoven's – and his own – behalf, writing to his London partner:

A most shabby figure you have made me out in this affair! – and that with one of the first composers of this day! You certainly might have found means in the course of two years and a half to have satisfied his demands! […] Don't lose a moment, then, pray, and send me word what you have received from him, that I may settle with him. 2

Clementi's editions of the Violin Concerto and its alternative piano version did eventually appear in London in 1810, but by then Beethoven had sanctioned publication by a Viennese publisher (Bureau des Arts et d'Industrie), which appeared in 1808. For research purposes, this remains the official first edition.

One probable reason why the concerto's first audiences found it so difficult to appreciate is that in many ways it signifies a remarkable break with tradition. The violin concertos of Mozart and Haydn for example are relatively short and much lighter in style and orchestration. With a playing time of around 45 minutes, Beethoven's Violin Concerto is significantly longer than any of his previous concertos: indeed, in most performances the first movement alone is as long as any of Mozart's first four violin concertos *in toto*, and only a few minutes shorter than K219. As in the Third Piano Concerto, Op. 37, Beethoven is clearly aiming here at a more symphonic style of concerto writing than important contemporaries like the Italian violinist-composer Giovanni Battista Viotti, some of whose 29 violin concertos Beethoven almost certainly knew.[3] The use of martial trumpets and drums – an invariable component in the orchestral line-up of Beethoven's symphonies – also sets the work apart in tone from Haydn's and Mozart's violin concertos.

There is one important respect in which Beethoven's Violin Concerto is more traditional than the Third Piano Concerto: the first movement's orchestral introduction features no modulations to other keys (though there are some dramatic major-minor contrasts). But Beethoven's presentation and development of his basic material is nevertheless comparable with that in his symphonic works, especially in its sophisticated use of what can seem startlingly simple motivic ingredients – could these be the 'commonplace' ideas whose 'repetition' the above-quoted Viennese reviewer had found 'wearisome'? The opening five drum-taps (on the tonic note D), for example, hardly seem like an idea at all in themselves; but this repeated note pattern, played by the first violins on a

2 See Alan Tyson, 'The Textual Problems of Beethoven's Violin Concerto', in *The Musical Quarterly*, Vol. 53, No. 4. (October 1967), 487. Tyson's article is of inestimable value in identifying the numerous corrupt passages in familiar editions of Beethoven's Violin Concerto.

3 For a discussion of the influence of the concertos of Viotti, and of other contemporary violinist-composers, on Beethoven's violin music in general, see Mark Kaplan, 'Beethoven's chamber music with piano', in *The Cambridge Companion to Beethoven* (Cambridge, 2000)

harmonically surprising and unresolved D♯ in bar 10, poses an immediate challenge to the stability of the home key, rather like the unexpected swing to C♯ in the first movement main theme of the 'Eroica' Symphony (Op. 55, I: bar 7). An echo of the Violin Concerto's destabilizing D♯ can be heard in the climactic E♭ (enharmonically D♯) of the first *fortissimo* tutti (I: bar 30), while the fully harmonized, melodically embellished D♯ – E progression in bars 65–68 (again on the five-note rhythmic pattern) can be heard as an attempt to rationalize this dissonant pitch within the context of the tonic D major.

After the soloist's entry in bar 90, Beethoven continues to use this basic repeated note pattern in ear-catching new ways. In bars 206–7 the first violins' repeated Es are answered by a subterranean F♮ from cellos and basses, *pianissimo*, the latter clashing perplexingly with the soloist's B–C♯ trill, three and a half octaves above. The contraction of the violin's trill to B–C♮ in bar 209, and the accompanying string writing in bars 210–11 do manage to make a kind of retrospective harmonic sense of this strange inspiration, but the effect of strangeness – of strained ambiguity – persists. Equally extraordinary is the widely spaced, skeletally harmonized progression f''' – G to $f♯'''$– $F♯$ in bars 299–300. The cellos and basses now use the initial repeated-note figure to emphasize F sharp as the dominant of a previously unprepared B minor. These could well be examples of the kind of 'broken' continuity that so perplexed the unnamed Viennese critic, but which are now so widely admired.

If this motif of five or four repeated notes seems to play a largely destabilizing role in the earlier stages of the first movement, as the recapitulation approaches its function becomes increasingly one of consolidation. Its appearance on horns at bar 330 *et seq* is the first time this figure has been heard entirely on the tonic D since the beginning of the solo exposition (bars 101–2). As such it represents a crucial foreshadowing of the recapitulation, which begins with a massive full-orchestral restatement of the original five-note figure at bars 365–6 – a function which can all too easily be obscured if (as happens all-too-frequently in performance) the soloist employs too much rubato at this point. In such passages one can, perhaps, begin to sympathize with the concerto's first audience in 1806. Listeners whose expectations were conditioned by the violin concertos of Viotti, or such other virtuoso-composers as Pierre Rode, Pierre Baillot or Rodolphe Kreutzer (dedicatee of Beethoven's Op. 47 Sonata) would have expected the soloist to be in the spotlight more or less throughout, with the violin part spectacular or melodically appealing enough in its own right, and with the orchestra mostly reduced to a merely supporting role. Beethoven's subtle interplay between soloist and orchestra created a kind of musical argument that may simply have been too complex for such an audience to grasp – in the face of which, to borrow a phrase form Samuel Johnson, 'the attention retires'.

Neither the *Larghetto* second movement nor the Rondo finale are as intellectually intricate as the concerto's monumental first movement. They are however impressive creations in their own right. The *Larghetto* is an imaginatively free set of variations on the theme presented by muted strings in bars 1–10. Note that this theme also offers a 'rationalization' of the first movement's destabilizing D sharp in bar 5, but now within the context of a serene, fundamentally secure G major. Beethoven also introduces a beautiful contrasting theme, still in G major, this time led melodically throughout by the soloist (II: bars 45-52 and again in bars 71-78). As in the first movement, a great deal of the solo violin writing is unusually high for its time, and Beethoven enhances its ethereal effect by keeping the orchestral writing as light and transparent as possible, with particularly sparing use of the bass instruments. This makes the final *fortissimo* string tutti (bars 89–91) – in which the mutes are removed for the first time – all the more dramatic, reinforcing the harmonic preparation for the return to D major in the finale.

The Rondo finale is, for the most part, easy to follow formally, and now the soloist is allowed more opportunities for pure virtuoso display, as in the magisterial two-part writing in bars 64–7, or the scintillating semiquaver chordal passage-work that follows. There is however one significant departure from normal concerto practice after the final cadenza (III: bar 280 *et seq*). (Beethoven left no written cadenzas for this concerto, and unfortunately the cadenzas he provided for the piano version of Op. 61 do not translate readily into violin writing.) In bar 280 the soloist comes to rest on a trill on the supertonic, E – fairly standard practice at the time; but the orchestra now begins a series of mysterious, tonally ambiguous rising figures, *diminuendo*, outlining a diminished seventh, and eventually settling in A flat major – the ultimate tonal extreme from the tonic D major. If it is the orchestra that leads the music away from D, it is the soloist who leads the way back, finally arriving there – after an elaborate triumphal flourish (though still *pianissimo*) – in bar 315. The orchestra destabilizes; the soloist restores order. The effect is seriously undermined if the previous solo cadenza in any way anticipates this wonderful harmonic departure and return.

This strikingly symphonic use of tonal argument and thematic development – along with the dramatization of the relationship between soloist and orchestra – is typical of Beethoven's mature concertos in general. But while in his piano concertos this transformation of the concerto style was to some extent anticipated by Mozart – especially in the latter's K466, K491 and K503 – in the Violin Concerto it is unprecedented. However slow audiences may have been at first to appreciate its greatness, its subsequent influence has been colossal. Mendelssohn's E minor Violin Concerto clearly owes a great deal to Beethoven's example; it is worth noting that Mendelssohn composed it immediately after his visit to London in 1844, during which he conducted that ground-breaking performance of the Beethoven concerto mentioned above. Likewise the grandly symphonic violin concertos of Brahms (1878), Sibelius (1905), Elgar (1910), Nielsen (1911), Schoenberg (1936), Britten (1939) and Shostakovich (1948 and 1967), different as they are, all establish themselves within a tradition created by Beethoven in his Op. 61.

Stephen Johnson

VORWORT

Beethovens Violinkonzert in D-Dur gilt seit langem als eine der größten Herausforderungen des Violinkonzert-Repertoires: als Prüfstein für künstlerische Reife wie technische Meisterschaft und somit als ein Werk, das jeder Virtuose, der den Namen verdient, auf irgendeiner Sprosse seiner Karriereleiter beherrschen sollte. Mithin mag es überraschen, wenn man entdeckt, wie kühl das Werk bei seiner Uraufführung in Wien am 23. Dezember 1806 aufgenommen wurde. Womöglich war es Wunschdenken, was den Komponisten und großen Bewunderer Beethovens Carl Czerny zu dem Bericht bewog, das Konzert sei „mit grösster Wirkung produziert worden."[1] Aller Wahrscheinlichkeit nach galt der Beifall eher dem Solisten, dem brillanten Franz Clement, der den überaus schwierigen und höchstwahrscheinlich vielfach korrigierten Violinpart mit großem Aplomb faktisch vom Blatt spielte und zwischen zwei Sätzen eine eigene, stupende Improvisation einfügte (bei der er offensichtlich die Geige umgekehrt hielt). Die allgemeine Reaktion auf Beethovens Musik wird wahrscheinlich besser von einer Kritik zusammengefasst, die am 8. Januar 1807 in der Wiener *Zeitung für Theater, Musik und Poesie* erschien:

Das Urtheil von Kennern [...] gesteht demselben manche Schönheit zu, bekennt aber, dass der Zusammenhang oft ganz zerrissen scheine, und die unendlichen Wiederholungen einiger gemeinen Stellen leicht ermüden könnten. Es sagt, dass Beethhofen [sic] seine anerkannt grossen Talente, gehöriger verwenden, und uns Werke schenken möge, die seinen ersten Symphonien aus C und D gleichen, seinem anmuthigen Septette aus Es [...].

Diese oder vergleichbare Auffassungen scheinen vorherrschend gewesen zu sein in jenen folgenden knapp vier Jahrzehnten, in denen die Aufführungszahlen des Violinkonzerts kaum je zweistellige Ziffern erreichten. Erst als der 13-jährige Joseph Joachim der einmal einer der legendären Violinvirtuosen des 19. Jahrhunderts werden sollte das Werk 1844 in einem Londoner Konzert unter der Stabführung Mendelssohns spielte, begann das breitere musikalische Publikum schließlich die herausragenden Qualitäten des Opus 61 zu erkennen. Was Beethoven von Clements Spiel hielt, ist nicht überliefert; möglicherweise spiegeln sich seine Empfindungen jedoch in der andernfalls unerklärlichen Widmungsänderung des Konzerts wider. Auf der ersten Seite des Autographs steht, in knorrigem, typisch Beethovenschem Wortwitz: „Concerto par Clemenza pour Clement primo Violino e direttore al theatro a vienna". Als 1808 jedoch die Partitur im Druck erschien, trug sie eine Widmung an Beethovens Jugendfreund Stephan von Breuning. Bemerkenswert ist ferner, dass von Beethoven kein Vorsatz überliefert ist, je wieder ein Violinkonzert schreiben zu wollen, und dass auch seine Produktion von Violinsonaten nach 1806 unübersehbar versiegt. Neun Sonaten für Violine und Klavier darunter als letzte die berühmte „Kreutzer"-Sonate Op. 47 von 1802/03 erschienen vor dem Konzert; danach komponierte Beethoven nur noch ein Werk für Solovioline: die Sonate G-Dur Op. 96 (1812, revidiert 1815). Letztere wird weithin für eines von Beethovens feinsten Kammermusikwerken mit Klavier angesehen, doch der Violinpart ist, anders als in der „Kreutzer"-Sonate oder in den Ecksätzen des Violinkonzerts, deutlich weniger virtuos, eher in einem lyrisch-kontemplativen Ton gehalten.

Sieht man von Carl Czerny ab, gab es zugunsten des Violinkonzerts mindestens eine weitere frühe, ermutigende Stimme. Im April 1807 erhielt Beethoven Besuch von dem Pianisten, Komponisten und Leiter eines Londoner Verlagshauses Muzio Clementi, der seiner Firma die englischen Rechte an einigen von Beethovens neuesten Werken sichern wollte. Diese schlossen das 4. Klavierkonzert Op. 58, die drei „Rasumowsky"-Quartette Op. 59, die 4. Sinfo-

[1] Carl Czerny: *Pianoforte-Schule*, Op. 500, IV, S. 117.

nie Op. 60 und die *Coriolan*-Ouvertüre Op. 62 ein. Aus seiner Korrespondenz erhellt, dass Clementi dem Violinkonzert besonderes Lob zollte; indes äußerte er auch eine im Rückblick sonderbar anmutende Bitte: Ob Beethoven nicht von dem Violinkonzert ein Arrangement für Klavier und Orchester anfertigen könne? Dieses erschien dann auch, mit derselben Opuszahl wie die Fassung für Violine, und trug eine Widmung an Stephan von Breunings Gattin Julie. Nun waren im 18. und frühen 19. Jahrhundert Arrangements von Konzerten für andere Soloinstrumente keineswegs ungewöhnlich, doch die Bearbeitung des Soloviolinparts von Opus 61, die mit an Sicherheit grenzender Wahrscheinlichkeit in Beethovens Auftrag von jemand anderem vorgenommen wurde, der einigen Vorschlägen folgte, die der Komponist ins Autograph gekritzelt hatte, trug nicht dazu bei, den Ruf des Konzerts zu retten. Tatsächlich handelt es sich um eine bemerkenswert einfallslose, bisweilen geradezu unbeholfene Adaption, in welcher der linken Hand kaum mehr zu tun bleibt, als die melodieführende Rechte zu begleiten. Das intrikate oder dramatische Wechselspiel zwischen den Händen, wie es für den Solostil in Beethovens fünf Klavierkonzerten so charakteristisch ist, fehlt fast gänzlich.

Jedenfalls wurde die Milch dieses anfangs so attraktiven Handels mit Clementi zuletzt sauer. Bis Ende 1809 war noch keines der o. g. Werke in England im Druck erschienen und kein Honorar ausgezahlt worden. Clementi, weiterhin auf dem Kontinent in Geschäften unterwegs, geriet schließlich um Beethovens und seiner eigenen Interessen willen in Rage, als er an seinen Londoner Compagnon schrieb:

In dieser Angelegenheit mache ich jetzt Ihretwegen eine höchst <u>schäbige</u> Figur! und dies in den Augen eines der <u>führenden</u> Komponisten unserer Tage! Bestimmt hätten Sie im Laufe von <u>zwei und ein halb Jahren</u> Mittel auftreiben können, seine Forderungen zu erfüllen! […] Säumen Sie also keinen Augenblick, bitte!, und geben Sie mir Bescheid, <u>was</u> Sie von ihm

erhalten haben, damit ich mich mit ihm ins Benehmen setze. [2]

Clementis Ausgaben des Violinkonzerts und seiner alternativen Fassung für Klavier erschienen schließlich in London 1810, doch zuvor hatte sich Beethoven bereits mit einem Wiener Verlagshaus (Bureau des Arts et d'Industrie/ Kunst- und Industriekontor) auf eine Ausgabe geeinigt, die 1808 im Druck erschien. Für Forschungszwecke bleibt diese die offizielle Erstausgabe. Ein wahrscheinlicher Grund dafür, warum sich die ersten Zuhörer mit der Wertschätzung des Konzerts so schwer taten, besteht darin, dass es in mehrfacher Hinsicht einen bemerkenswerten Bruch mit der Tradition markiert. Die Violinkonzerte von Mozart und Haydn z. B. sind relativ kurz und in Stil und Instrumentation viel leichtgewichtiger. Mit einer Aufführungsdauer von etwa 45 Minuten ist Beethovens Violinkonzert bedeutend länger als irgendeines seiner Vorgänger-Werke; ja, bei den meisten Aufführungen ist der erste Satz allein schon eben so lang wie eines der ersten vier Mozart-Konzerte *in toto* und nur wenige Minuten kürzer als das A-Dur-Konzert KV 219. Wie im 3. Klavierkonzert Op. 37 zielt Beethoven hier unübersehbar auf einen Stil konzertanten Komponierens, der sinfonischer sein sollte als bei so bedeutenden Zeitgenossen wie etwa dem italienischen Geiger-Komponisten Giovanni Battista Viotti, von dessen 29 Violinkonzerten Beethoven fast sicher einige kannte.[3] Auch mit der Verwendung von martialisch tönenden Trompeten und Pauken – unveränderliche Bestandteile der Instrumentation von Beethovens Sinfonien – setzt sich das Werk im Klang von den Violinkonzerten Haydns und Mozarts deutlich ab.

In einem wichtigen Aspekt jedoch ist Beethovens Violinkonzert traditioneller als das dritte

[2] Siehe Alan Tyson: „The Textual Problems of Beethoven's Violin Concerto", in *The Musical Quarterly*, Bd. 53, Nr. 4. (Oktober 1967), S. 487. Tysons Artikel ist sehr wertvoll, um die zahlreichen korrumpierten Stellen in bekannten Ausgaben von Beethovens Violinkonzert identifizieren zu können.

[3] Zu Beethovens Violinmusik im Allgemeinen und zum Einfluss der Konzerte von Viotti und anderer zeitgenössischer Geiger-Komponisten siehe Mark Kaplan: „Beethoven's chamber music with piano", in *The Cambridge Companion to Beethoven*, Cambridge 2000.

Klavierkonzert: Die Orchestereinleitung im ersten Satz enthält keine Modulationen in andere Tonarten (auch wenn es einige dramatische Dur-Moll-Kontraste gibt). Indes ist Beethovens Einführung und Fortspinnung seines Ausgangsmaterials nichtsdestoweniger mit denen seiner sinfonischen Werke vergleichbar, zumal in seiner raffinierten Verwendung dessen, was als motivische Ingredienzien von bestürzender Simplizität scheinen mag: Sollte es sich bei diesen etwa um jene „gemeinen" Stellen handeln, deren „unendliche Wiederholungen" nach dem Urteil des o. g. Wiener Kritikers „leicht ermüden" könnten? Die eröffnenden fünf Pauken-Viertel im *piano* auf dem Grundton D zum Beispiel haben an sich kaum motivische Dignität und doch stellt diese repetitive Gestalt, wenn sie von den ersten Violinen in Takt 10 auf einem harmonisch überraschenden und unaufgelösten Dis gespielt wird, sogleich die Stabilität der Grundtonart in Frage, nicht unähnlich der unerwarteten Ausweichung nach Cis im Hauptthema des 1. Satzes der „Eroica" Op. 55, Takt 7. Ein Echo auf dieses destabilisierende Dis im Violinkonzert ist im Es (enharmonisch Dis) auf der Klimax des ersten Tutti-Fortissimos im 1. Satz, Takt 30 zu vernehmen, während die voll ausharmonisierte, melodisch figurierte Dis-E-Fortschreitung in den Takten 65–68 (wieder auf jenem fünftönigen rhythmischen *pattern*) als Versuch gehört werden kann, diese dissonante Tonstufe in ein sinnvolles Verhältnis zum Kontext des tonalen D-Dur zu setzen.

Nach dem Einsatz des Solisten in Takt 90 fährt Beethoven damit fort, jenes repetitive Klopfmotiv auf neue Weise dem Ohr sinnfällig zu machen. In Takt 206-207 wird das repetierte Es in den ersten Violinen von einem aus der Tiefe herauftönenden *Pianissimo*-F in den Celli und Bässen beantwortet, wobei letzteres auf verstörende Weise an dem harschen H-Cis-Triller, dreieinhalb Oktaven höher, sich reibt. Der Verengung des Geigentrillers in Takt 209 zu H-C und dem begleitenden Streichersatz in den Takten 210–211 gelingt es, diese eigenartige Eingebung, quasi rückblickend, harmonisch plausibel zu machen, doch der Verfremdungs-effekt – der Eindruck einer angespannten Mehrdeutigkeit – bleibt bestehen. Ebenso außergewöhnlich ist die weiträumige, nur karg harmonisierte Fortschreitung *f'''-G* zu *fis'''-Fis* in T. 299–300. Celli und Bässe verwenden hier die repetitive Anfangsgestalt zur Akzentuierung von Fis als Dominante eines zuvor unvorbereiteten h-Moll. Diese Stellen könnten gut als Beispiele für jene „gebrochene" Kontinuität einstehen, die den anonymen Wiener Kritiker so verstörte, Stellen, die heute indes weithin bewundert werden.

Während dieses Motiv aus vier oder fünf repetierten Tönen in den früheren Stadien des ersten Satzes eine zumeist destabilisierende Rolle zu spielen scheint, wird seine Funktion beim Näherrücken der Reprise in wachsendem Maße eine der Konsolidierung. Bei seinem Erscheinen in den Hörnern in Takt 330f. geschieht es zum ersten Mal, dass es, seit dem Beginn der Soloexposition (T. 101–102), vollständig in der Tonika D zu vernehmen ist. Hierbei repräsentiert es eine entscheidende Vorahnung der Reprise, die in Takt 365–366 mit einer massiven Wiederbekräftigung der ursprünglichen fünftönigen Gestalt im vollen Orchester einsetzt – eine Funktion, die nur zu leicht verdunkelt werden kann, wenn der Solist (wie es allzu oft bei Aufführungen geschieht) an dieser Stelle zuviel Rubato verwendet. Aus solchen Passagen kann man vielleicht einen Anflug von Verständnis für das Uraufführungs-Publikum von 1806 gewinnen. Hörer, deren Erwartungen von den Violinkonzerten Viottis oder solcher Virtuosen-Komponisten wie Pierre Rode, Pierre Baillot oder Rodolphe Kreutzer (dem Widmungsträger von Beethovens Sonate Op. 47) geprägt waren, hätten erwartet, dass der Solist mehr oder weniger ständig an der Rampe des musikalischen Geschehens stünde, indem der Violinpart als solcher bereits spektakulär oder eingängig genug und das Orchester vorwiegend auf eine stützende Rolle beschränkt wäre. Beethovens subtiles Wechselspiel zwischen Solist und Orchester erschuf eine Art musikalischen Dialog, der schlechterdings zu komplex gewesen sein mochte, als dass das Publikum ihm hätte folgen können – in dessen Mienen, um eine Wendung Samuel Johnsons zu entlehnen, „die Aufmerksamkeit sich zurücke zieht".

Weder der 2. Satz (*Larghetto*) noch das Rondo-Finale sind gedanklich so intrikat wie der monumentale Eingangssatz des Konzerts. Dennoch sind sie eindrucksvolle Gebilde sui generis. Das *Larghetto* ist eine fantasievoll freie Folge von Variationen über das Thema, das in Takt 110 von sordinierten Streichern vorgestellt wird. Man beachte, dass dieses Thema in Takt 5 ebenfalls eine „Sinnfälligmachung" des destabilisierenden Dis aus dem ersten Satz bietet, nun aber im Kontext eines abendschönen, grundtönig gesicherten G-Dur. Beethoven führt auch ein wundervolles Kontrastthema ein, das diesmal, weiterhin in G-Dur, vom Solisten durchgängig melodisch geführt wird (II. Satz: Takt 45–52 und wieder in T. 71–78). Wie im 1. Satz liegt die Soloviolinstimme zu großen Teilen in – für ihre Zeit – ungewöhnlich hoher Lage und Beethoven verstärkt diese ätherische Wirkung noch, indem er den Orchestersatz so schwerelos und transparent wie möglich hält, mit besonders sparsamem Gebrauch der Bassinstrumente. Dies macht das Streichertutti-*Fortissimo* am Schluss (T. 89–91) – bei dem die Dämpfer zum ersten Mal in diesem Satz entfernt werden – um so dramatischer, wobei es die harmonische Vorbereitung zur Rückkehr nach D-Dur im Finale bekräftigt. Dem Rondo-Finale ist formal meistenteils unschwer zu folgen und dem Solisten werden jetzt mehr Gelegenheiten zur Ausstellung reiner Virtuosität zugestanden, wie etwa in den herrischen Doppelgriffen in Takt 64–67 oder in dem funkelnden Sechzehntelpassagenwerk, das darauf folgt. Eine bezeichnende Abweichung von der normalen Konzertpraxis jedoch findet sich nach der Schlusskadenz in Takt 280f. (Beeethoven hinterließ für dieses Konzert keine ausgeschriebenen Kadenzen und leider lassen sich die Kadenzen, die er für die Klavierfassung des Opus 61 besorgte, ins Idiom der Geige nicht gut übertragen). In Takt 280 gelangt der Solist zu einem Halt auf einem Triller auf der II. (Oberdominant-)Stufe E: die übliche Standardpraxis seinerzeit – doch das Orchester setzt nun mit einer Folge geheimnisvoller, tonal mehrdeutiger aufsteigender Figuren ein, *diminuendo*, erst im Umriss einer verminderten Sept, schließlich auf As-Dur sich festsetzend, der von der Tonika D-Dur am äußersten entfernten Stufe. Wenn es Sache des Orchesters war, die Musik von D-Dur zu entfernen, ist es nun am Solisten, den Weg zurückzufinden, indem er – nach elaboriert triumphalen, bravourösen Läufen (wiewohl immer noch pianissimo) – in Takt 315 schließlich wieder in D-Dur ankommt. Das Orchester destabilisiert – der Solist stellt wieder Ordnung her. Diese Wirkung wird ernstlich in Frage gestellt, wenn die vorausgehende Solokadenz auf irgendeine Weise jene wundervolle harmonische Ausfahrt und Heimkehr vorwegnimmt.

Diese frappierend sinfonische Verwendung von Dialog und thematischer Durchführung – im Verein mit der Dramatisierung der Beziehung zwischen Solist und Orchester – ist generell kennzeichnend für Beethovens reife Konzerte. Doch während in seinen Klavierkonzerten diese Transformation des konzertanten Stils bis zu einem gewissen Grade von Mozart vorweggenommen worden war – besonders in dessen späten Klavierkonzerten KV 466, 491 und 503 –, hat sie im Violinkonzert keine Präzedenz. Wie schwer es zu Anfang den Zuhörern auch gefallen sein mochte, dessen Größe anzuerkennen – sein Einfluss in der Folgezeit war kolossal. Mendelssohns großes e-Moll-Violinkonzert ist Beethovens Vorbild deutlich verpflichtet; man sollte nicht übersehen, dass Mendelssohn es unmittelbar nach seinem Londoner Besuch von 1844 komponierte, bei dem er jene eingangs erwähnte Aufführung des Beethoven-Konzerts dirigierte, das den Bann, der über dem Werk gelegen hatte, schließlich brach. Ebenso fügen sich die großsinfonischen Violinkonzerte von Brahms (1879), Sibelius (1905), Elgar (1910), Nielsen (1911), Schönberg (1936), Britten (1939) und Schostakowitsch (1948 & 1967), so verschieden sie auch sind, allesamt in eine Tradition, die von Beethoven mit seinem Opus 61 ihre Gründungsurkunde erhielt.

Stephen Johnson
Übersetzung: Wolfgang Schlüter

PRÉFACE

Le Concerto pour violon en *ré* majeur de Beethoven est réputé de longue date pour l'un des plus grands défis du répertoire pour violon solo. Epreuve tant de maturité artistique que de maîtrise technique, c'est une œuvre que tout virtuose digne de ce nom se doit de posséder au cours de sa carrière. Il est donc surprenant de découvrir qu'elle reçut un accueil réservé lors de sa création à Vienne, le 23 décembre 1806. Le compositeur Carl Czerny, grand admirateur de Beethoven, n'exprima peut-être qu'un vœu pieux en affirmant que le concerto « fut donné avec grand effet »[1]. Selon toute vraisemblance, les applaudissements s'adressèrent plus au soliste, le brillant Franz Clement, qui déchiffra pratiquement la partie de violon, certainement très retouchée et d'une extraordinaire difficulté, avec une superbe assurance et y ajouta une étincelante improvisation (tenant apparemment son violon à l'envers à un certain moment) entre deux des mouvements. Une critique parue dans le journal viennois *Zeitung für Theater, Musik und Poesie* du 8 janvier 1807 résume sans doute bien la réaction générale vis-à-vis de l'œuvre de Beethoven.

Quant au concerto de Beethhofen [*sic*], le verdict des connaisseurs est unanime. Ceux-ci lui concèdent une certaine beauté mais maintiennent que la continuité y apparaît souvent complètement brisée et que la répétition incessante de certains passages banals peut vite s'avérer fastidieuse. Ils déclarent que Beethhofen pourrait mieux utiliser son indiscutable immense talent et nous proposer plus d'œuvres de la veine de ses symphonies en *ut* et en *ré*, de son délicieux Septuor en *mi* bémol […]

Cette opinion prévalut, à peu de choses près, durant presque quatre décennies, au cours desquelles le nombre des exécutions du Concerto pour violon atteignit à peine dix. Ce ne fut que lorsque le jeune Joseph Joachim – qui allait devenir l'un des violonistes virtuoses légendaires du XIXe siècle –, alors âgé de treize ans, le joua

pendant un concert à Londres en 1844, sous la direction de Mendelssohn, que les qualités extraordinaires du concerto commencèrent enfin à être reconnues par un auditoire musical élargi.

Le jugement de Beethoven sur l'interprétation de Clement n'a pas été consigné, mais il se peut que son sentiment se reflète dans le changement, inexpliqué par ailleurs, de la dédicace du concerto. La première page du manuscrit autographe, dans la ligne du goût de Beethoven pour les jeux de mots, porte l'inscription : « Concerto par Clemenza pour Clement primo Violino e direttore al theatro a vienna », or la partition fut publiée en 1808 avec une dédicace à Stephan von Breuning, ami d'enfance de Beethoven. On remarque également que Beethoven ne manifesta jamais le désir d'écrire un autre concerto pour violon et que sa production de sonates pour violon cessa significativement après 1806. Neuf sonates pour violon et piano – dont la célèbre et dernière Sonate « à Kreutzer », Op. 47, de 1802/03 – parurent avant le concerto qui ne fut suivi que d'une seule œuvre pour violon solo, la Sonate en *sol*, Op. 96 (1812, révisée en 1815). Cette dernière est largement considérée comme l'une des plus belles œuvres de chambre avec piano de Beethoven. L'écriture de la partie de violon y est nettement moins virtuose et d'une veine plus lyrique et contemplative que celle de la Sonate « A Kreutzer » ou celle des mouvements extrêmes du Concerto pour violon.

A côté de Czerny, une autre voix au moins estima favorablement le Concerto pour violon. En avril 1807, Beethoven reçut la visite du pianiste, compositeur et directeur d'une maison d'édition anglaise Muzio Clementi, soucieux d'obtenir les droits pour l'Angleterre de quelques œuvres récentes de Beethoven, parmi lesquelles figuraient le Quatrième Concerto pour piano, Op. 58, les trois quatuors à cordes « Razumowsky », Op. 59, la Symphonie No 4, Op. 60 et l'Ouverture de *Coriolan*, Op. 62. Dans sa correspondance, Clementi loua particulièrement le

[1] Carl Czerny, *Pianoforte-Schule*, Op. 500, IV, p.117

Concerto pour violon, assortissant son éloge d'une demande qui, avec le recul, paraît étrange : Beethoven accepterait-il également de réaliser un arrangement du Concerto pour violon pour piano et orchestre ? Cet arrangement parut en bonne et due forme, sous le même numéro d'*opus* que la version pour violon et portant une dédicace à l'épouse de Stephan von Breuning, Julie. Les adaptations de concertos pour d'autres instruments solistes n'étaient aucunement inhabituelles au XVIIIe siècle et au début du XIXe siècle mais la réécriture de la partie de violon de l'Op. 61 – sûrement effectuée par quelqu'un d'autre que Beethoven en suivant quelques indications gribouillées sur le manuscrit autographe par le compositeur – ne sauva pas la réputation du concerto. Il s'agit, en fait, d'une adaptation notoirement dénuée d'imagination et parfois fort maladroite dans laquelle la main gauche ne fait, à peu près, qu'accompagner la ligne dominante de la main droite. L'interaction complexe ou dramatique entre les deux mains, signature du style du soliste de ses cinq concertos pour pianos numérotés, y manque presque totalement.

En tout état de cause, la transaction avec Clementi, qui, de prime abord, paraissait prometteuse, se passa mal. A la fin de 1809, aucune des œuvres citées plus haut n'avaient été imprimées en Angleterre et aucun paiement n'avait été honoré. Clementi, qui travaillait encore sur le Continent, furieux au nom de Beethoven et en son nom propre, écrivit à son associé londonien :

Vous m'avez fait passer pour un personnage des plus <u>misérables</u> dans cette affaire ! – et ce auprès de l'un des <u>premiers</u> compositeurs d'aujourd'hui ! Vous auriez certainement dû trouver le moyen en <u>deux ans et demi</u> de satisfaire sa demande ! [...] Ne perdez plus un moment, s'il vous plaît. Envoyez-moi <u>tout</u> ce que vous avez reçu de lui, de manière à ce que je puisse m'arranger avec lui.[2]

Finalement, Clementi fit paraître les éditions du Concerto pour violon et de sa version pour piano à Londres en 1810, alors que Beethoven avait déjà autorisé leur publication par un éditeur viennois (Bureau des Arts et d'Industrie) qui parut en 1808 et demeure la première édition officielle de l'œuvre du point de vue de la recherche.

Une des raisons probables de la difficulté d'appréciation du concerto par ses premiers auditeurs réside dans le fait qu'il rompt de façon éclatante et multiple avec la tradition. Les concertos pour violon de Mozart et de Haydn, par exemple, sont relativement courts et présentent un style et une orchestration beaucoup plus légers. D'une durée d'environ quarante-cinq minutes, le Concerto pour violon de Beethoven est considérablement plus long que tous ses concertos précédents. De plus, l'exécution de son seul premier mouvement est en général aussi longue que celle de l'intégralité de l'un ou l'autre des quatre premiers concertos pour violon de Mozart et ne dure que quelques minutes de moins que celle du K. 219. De même que dans son Troisième Concerto pour piano, Op. 37, Beethoven recherche ici un style d'écriture concertante plus symphonique que celui d'éminents compositeurs contemporains comme le violoniste et compositeur italien Giovanni Battista Viotti dont Beethoven connaissait sûrement les vingt-neuf concertos pour violon.[3] Le recours aux trompettes et aux percussions martiales, composante permanente de la formation orchestrale des symphonies de Beethoven, éloigne également l'œuvre de l'univers sonore des concertos pour violons de Haydn et de Mozart.

Si le Concerto pour violon de Beethoven se révèle, toutefois, plus traditionnel que son Troisième Concerto pour piano par la notable absence de modulation dans l'introduction orchestrale de son premier mouvement (malgré quelques effets spectaculaires d'opposition entre modes majeur et mineur), l'exposition et le développement des éléments constitutifs fon-

---

2 Voir Alan Tyson, « The Textual Problems of Beethoven's Violin Concerto », dans *The Musical Quarterly*, vol. 53, Nº 4 (octobre 1967), p.487. L'article de Tyson est d'une valeur inestimable pour ses repérages des nombreux passages erronés des éditions connues du Concerto pour violon de Beethoven.

3 Sur l'influence des concertos de Viotti et d'autres violonistes compositeurs de l'époque et sur la musique pour violon de Beethoven en général, voir Mark Kaplan, « Beethoven's chamber music with piano », dans *The Cambridge Companion to Beethoven*, Cambridge, 2000

damentaux du Concerto pour violon sont comparables à ceux des œuvres symphoniques de Beethoven, surtout par leur recours complexe à des motifs originellement simples. S'agirait-il ici des idées « banales » dont la « répétition » parut « fastidieuse » au critique viennois cité ci-dessus ? Les cinq coups frappés aux timbales qui ouvrent l'œuvre (sur la tonique *ré*) ne semblent, par exemple, pas relever d'une idée musicale en eux-mêmes, mais ce motif de notes répétées, joué par les premiers violons sur une *ré* dièse à l'harmonie surprenante et non résolue à la mesure 10, pose un défi immédiat à la stabilité de la tonalité principale, à l'image du passage inattendu en *do* dièse du thème principal du premier mouvement de la Symphonie *Eroica* (Op. 55, I, mesure 7). On trouve un écho de ce *ré* dièse déstabilisateur dans l'arrivée sur *mi* bémol (enharmonique de *ré* dièse) du premier *tutti* d'orchestre *fortissimo* (I, mesure 30), tandis que l'enchaînement *ré* dièse-*mi* des mesures 65 à 68, pleinement harmonisé et orné mélodiquement (de nouveau sur le motif rythmique de cinq notes), se présente comme une tentative de rationalisation de cette dissonance dans le contexte de la tonalité de *ré* majeur de la tonique.

Après l'entrée du soliste à la mesure 90, Beethoven reprend constamment le motif de simples notes répétées de manière insolite. Dans les mesures 206 à 207, aux *mi* répétés des premiers violons répond le *fa* naturel profond des violoncelles et des contrebasses, dans la nuance *pianissimo*, qui se frotte avec équivoque au trille *si-do* dièse du soliste trois octaves et demie plus haut. La contraction du trille du violon sur *si-do* naturel à la mesure 209 et l'écriture des cordes qui l'accompagnent dans les mesures 210/211 parviennent à rendre un sens harmonique rétrospectif à cette singulière inspiration mais l'effet d'étrangeté – d'ambiguïté tendue – persiste. Tout aussi extraordinaire se révèle l'enchaînement largement espacé et à peine harmonisé superposant *fa*3 et *fa*3 dièse dans l'aigu et *sol* et *fa* dièse dans le grave des mesures 299/300. Les violoncelles et les contrebasses utilisent ici la formule de notes répétées initiale pour mettre en valeur *fa* dièse comme dominante du *si* mineur

non préparé précédemment. Ces exemples illustrent peut-être la continuité « brisée » qui déconcerta tant le critique viennois inconnu et qui est maintenant hautement admirée. Si ce motif de cinq ou quatre notes répétées joue un rôle très troublant dans le début du premier mouvement, à l'approche de la réexposition, sa fonction se transforme de plus en plus en celle de consolidation. Son apparition aux cors, à la mesure 330 sq., représente la première fois qu'on entend ce motif entièrement joué sur la tonique *ré* depuis le début de l'exposition du solo (mesures 101–102) et une préfiguration essentielle de la réexposition commençant par la réaffirmation puissante des cinq notes originales par le grand orchestre des mesures 365–366. Cette fonction peut être très facilement éclipsée si (comme c'est le cas dans de nombreuses interprétations) le soliste produit un trop grand *rubato* à cet endroit. Dans de tels passages, on peut comprendre le premier public du concerto en 1806 qui, formé aux concertos pour violon de Viotti ou aux virtuoses compositeurs tels que Pierre Rode, Pierre Baillot ou Rodolphe Kreutzer (dédicataire de la Sonate « à Kreutzer » de Beethoven), s'attendait à ce que le soliste soit mis en valeur d'un bout à l'autre de l'œuvre par une partie de violon spectaculaire ou mélodiquement attachante par elle-même, le rôle de l'orchestre étant réduit à celui de simple faire-valoir. L'interaction subtile élaborée par Beethoven entre le soliste et l'orchestre créait une sorte de rivalité musicale sans doute trop ardue pour ces auditeurs lorsqu'ils y furent confrontés, entraînant la réaction résumée par une formule empruntée à Samuel Johnson : « l'attention se relâche ».

Ni le deuxième mouvement *Larghetto*, ni le *Rondo finale* ne sont d'une conception intellectuelle aussi complexe que le premier mouvement monumental du concerto. Chacun d'eux représente néanmoins une création impressionnante. Le *Larghetto* est une série de variations libres et inventives sur un thème exposé par les cordes avec sourdine dans les mesures 1 à 10. On remarquera que ce thème offre une « rationalisation » du *ré* dièse irrésolu de la mesure 5, placé maintenant dans le contexte d'un *sol* majeur serein et fondamentalement sûr. Beethoven y introduit également un beau thème contrasté, toujours en *sol* majeur, cette fois constamment conduit mélodiquement par le soliste (II, mesures 45–52 et de nouveau dans les mesures 71-78). De même que dans le premier mouvement, une grande partie de la ligne de violon solo est écrite dans un aigu inhabituel pour son époque et Beethoven insiste sur son effet éthéré en maintenant l'écriture orchestrale aussi légère et transparente que possible par un recours particulièrement ténu aux instruments graves. Ceci rend le *fortissimo* final du *tutti* de cordes – sourdines enlevées pour la première fois – d'autant plus dramatique et renforce la préparation harmonique au retour du *ré* majeur du *finale*.

Le *Rondo finale* est d'une structure d'ensemble facile à suivre. Le soliste y croise de plus nombreuses occasions de pure virtuosité, comme dans le magistral passage à deux voix des mesures 64–67 ou la séquence éblouissante de doubles croches en accords qui le suit. Toutefois, ce mouvement s'écarte de la pratique usuelle du concerto après la cadence (III, mesure 280 *sq.*) (Beethoven n'a pas laissé de cadences pour ce concerto et les cadences qu'il fournit pour la version pour piano de l'Op. 61 ne s'adaptent malheureusement pas à l'écriture violonistique.) A la mesure 280, le soliste s'attarde sur un trille sur la sus-tonique *mi*, selon une pratique assez répandue à l'époque, alors que l'orchestre commence à enchaîner une série de configurations ascendantes *diminuendo* mystérieuses, de tonalité ambiguë, dessinant une septième diminuée avant de finalement atteindre la tonalité de *la* bémol majeur, ultime extrémité tonale de la tonalité fondamentale de *ré* majeur.

C'est l'orchestre qui détourne le discours musical de *ré*, c'est le soliste qui l'y ramène, après un exploit triomphal accompli (quoique toujours *pianissimo*) à la mesure 315. L'orchestre déséquilibre, le soliste restaure l'équilibre. Cet effet est sérieusement diminué si la cadence précédente anticipe d'une quelconque façon ce magnifique aller et retour harmonique.

Cette tournure symphonique frappante par la confrontation tonale et le développement thématique – allié à la dramatisation des rapports entre soliste et orchestre – est caractéristique des concertos de la maturité de Beethoven. Mais, tandis cette transformation du style du concerto fut, dans une certaine mesure, anticipée pour ses concertos pour piano par ceux de Mozart – en particulier dans les K.466, K.491 et K.503 – elle est sans précédent pour le Concerto pour violon. Quelle qu'ait été la résistance de ses auditoires à en apprécier d'emblée la grandeur, son influence ultérieure a été énorme. Le grand Concerto pour violon en *mi* mineur de Mendelssohn doit à l'évidence beaucoup au modèle de Beethoven. Il est à noter que Mendelssohn le composa immédiatement après sa visite à Londres, en 1844, durant laquelle il dirigea l'exécution décisive du Concerto de Beethoven mentionnée plus haut. Par ailleurs, les grands concertos symphoniques pour violon de Brahms (1878), Sibelius (1905), Elgar (1910), Nielsen (1911), Schoenberg (1936), Britten (1939) et Chostakovitch (1948 et 1967), aussi différents soient-ils, s'ancrent tous dans la tradition créée par Beethoven dans son Op. 61.

Stephen Johnson
Traduction : Agnès Ausseur

VIOLIN CONCERTO

Stephan von Breuning gewidmet

Ludwig van Beethoven
(1770–1827)
Op. 61

I. **Allegro ma non troppo**

No. 701   EE 7131

II. Larghetto

III. Rondo

243
Fg. 1
Cor (D) 1 2
Vl. pr.
I
Vl.
II
Vla.
Vc.
Cb.
p
248
Fl.
Ob. 1 2
Cl. (A) 1 2
Fg. 1 2
cresc.
f